W9-AQC-683

Date: 7/8/14

J 599.67 HAN
Hanson, Anders,
Elephant /

SandCastle™

Giant Animals

ELEPHANT

ANDERS HANSON

Consulting Editor, Diane Craig, M.A./Reading Specialist

A Division of ABDO

ABDO
Publishing Company

visit us at www.abdopublishing.com

Published by ABDO Publishing Company, a division of ABDO, P.O. Box 398166, Minneapolis, Minnesota 55439. Copyright © 2014 by Abdo Consulting Group, Inc. International copyrights reserved in all countries. No part of this book may be reproduced in any form without written permission from the publisher. SandCastle™ is a trademark and logo of ABDO Publishing Company.

Printed in the United States of America, North Mankato, Minnesota
102013
012014

 PRINTED ON RECYCLED PAPER

Editor: Liz Salzmann
Content Developer: Nancy Tuminelly
Cover and Interior Design and Production: Anders Hanson, Mighty Media, Inc.
Photo Credits: Shutterstock, Thinkstock

Library of Congress Cataloging-in-Publication Data
Hanson, Anders, 1980- author.
  Elephant / Anders Hanson ; consulting editor, Diane Craig, M.A., reading specialist.
    pages cm. -- (Giant animals)
  Audience: 4 to 9.
  ISBN 978-1-62403-057-4
1. Elephants--Juvenile literature. I. Craig, Diane, editor. II. Title.
  QL737.P98H362 2014
  599.67--dc23
                      2013023926

SandCastle™ Level: Transitional

SandCastle™ books are created by a team of professional educators, reading specialists, and content developers around five essential components—phonemic awareness, phonics, vocabulary, text comprehension, and fluency—to assist young readers as they develop reading skills and strategies and increase their general knowledge. All books are written, reviewed, and leveled for guided reading, early reading intervention, and Accelerated Reader® programs for use in shared, guided, and independent reading and writing activities to support a balanced approach to literacy instruction. The SandCastle™ series has four levels that correspond to early literacy development. The levels are provided to help teachers and parents select appropriate books for young readers.

Emerging Readers
(no flags)

Beginning Readers
(1 flag)

Transitional Readers
(2 flags)

Fluent Readers
(3 flags)

contents

HELLO, ELEPHANT!

ELEPHANT, 13 FEET (4 M)

Elephants are huge **mammals**. They are the biggest land animals on Earth! Elephants grow up to 13 feet (4 m) tall. They weigh up to 15,000 pounds (6,804 kg).

Elephants have long noses. They are called trunks. Elephants also have giant teeth that stick out. These huge teeth are called tusks.

tusks

trunk

HUMAN, 6 FEET (1.8 M)

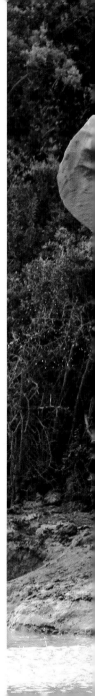

WHAT A NOSE!

Elephants can do a lot with their trunks! They use them to **smell** and hold things. They can also spray water with their trunks.

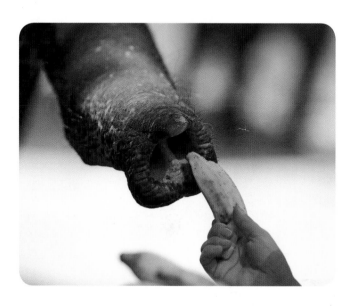

WHAT DO YOU EAT?

Elephants are plant eaters.

They eat leaves, **bark**, and grass.

BIG TUSKS!

Elephant tusks are really long teeth! Elephants use them to dig. They can also pull off tree **bark**. **Male** elephants use their tusks in fights.

DO YOU HAVE A FAMILY?

Elephants have one calf at a time. Calves weigh about 250 pounds (115 kg) at **birth**!

DO YOU HAVE FRIENDS?

Female and young elephants live in large herds. **Male** elephants live alone.

YOU'RE WRINKLY!

Elephants have gray, **wrinkled** skin. It's about 1 inch (2.5 cm) thick!

WHERE DO YOU LIVE?

There are two types of elephants. African elephants are bigger. They live in Africa. Asian elephants are smaller. They live in Asia.

AFRICAN ELEPHANT

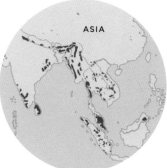

ASIAN ELEPHANT

ARE YOU SMART?

Elephants are smart.
They can use tools.
Some elephants have
even learned to paint!

QUICK QUIZ

Check your answers below!

1. Elephants are the biggest land animals.
   TRUE OR FALSE?

2. Elephants use their tusks to eat.
   TRUE OR FALSE?

3. Elephants have smooth skin.
   TRUE OR FALSE?

4. Elephants only live in Africa.
   TRUE OR FALSE?

1) True 2) False 3) False 4) False

GLOSSARY

bark – the covering or skin of a tree trunk or branch.

birth – the moment when a person or animal is born.

female – being of the sex that can produce eggs or give birth. Mothers are female.

male – being of the sex that can father offspring. Fathers are male.

mammal – a warm-blooded animal that has hair and whose females produce milk to feed their young.

smell – to sense an odor or scent.

wrinkled – having many wrinkles, or small folds.